STORY MONSTERS APPROVED

Published by
Adventuresome Words
Northumberland
England
www.adventuresomewords.com
info@adventuresomewords.com

First published by Adventuresome Words in 2023.
Text and illustrations copyright © Dr K. P. George 2023.
Illustrator: Laura Mocelin.

All rights reserved. This book or parts thereof may not be reproduced in any form, stored in any retrieval system, or transmitted in any form by any means; electronic, mechanical, photocopy, recording, or otherwise, without prior written permission of the publisher. This includes the use of this work by artificial intelligence systems for purposes such as training, data mining, or content generation. Unauthorised use by AI models or platforms is strictly prohibited.

Dr K. P. George
Landmarks on the Move
ISBN: 978-1-7384405-1-1

This book belongs to
_____
_____

LANDMARKS
ON THE MOVE

To you, little explorer,

As you read this book, remember that every day is an adventure waiting to be discovered.

Just like the landmarks that travel the world, you can explore, learn, and enjoy the wonders of our beautiful planet.

Happy reading and happy adventures!

Once upon a time, in a land far, far away,
The Eiffel Tower grumbled and had nothing to say.

Life in Paris was as dull as a butter knife,
Tourists were all glued to screens, not noticing his life.

"Hey, little birdie, know any calm and quiet spots?
Somewhere for a bit of yoga and grass with peaceful thoughts?"

Birdie chirped and shared the news that was quite profound,
The Buddha statue in Sri Lanka was London-bound!

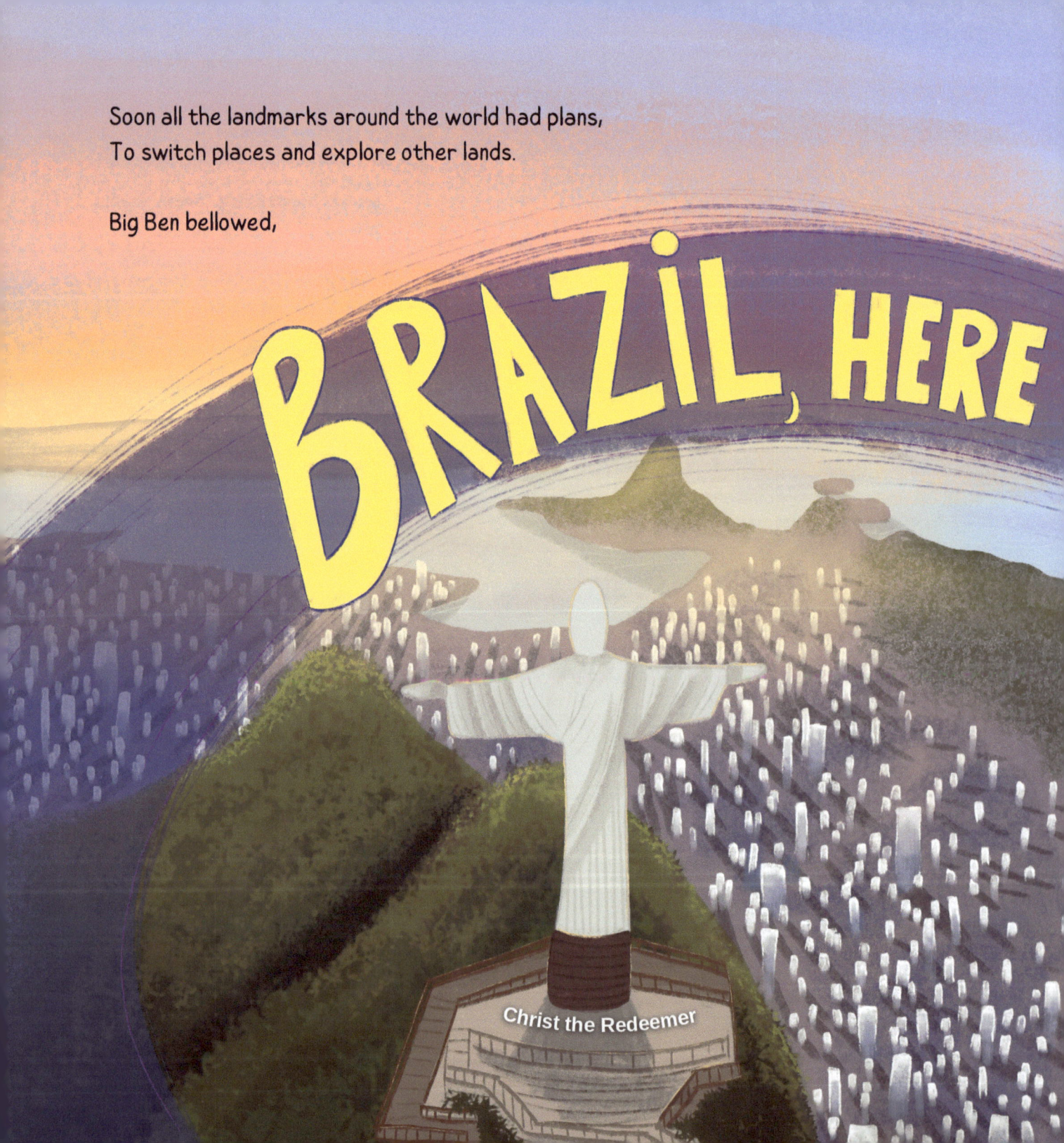

Soon all the landmarks around the world had plans,
To switch places and explore other lands.

Big Ben bellowed,

BRAZIL, HERE

Christ the Redeemer

*The tower's name is 'Elisabeth Tower,' that's true,
But many say 'Big Ben,' and that's not new.

'Big Ben' is the bell that rings with a clue,
Like renaming a toy or pet, it's something we do!*

But no adult noticed the landmarks had switched,
Only children saw the magic that had been stitched.

Golden Gate Bridge

They connected and worked with a plan in mind,

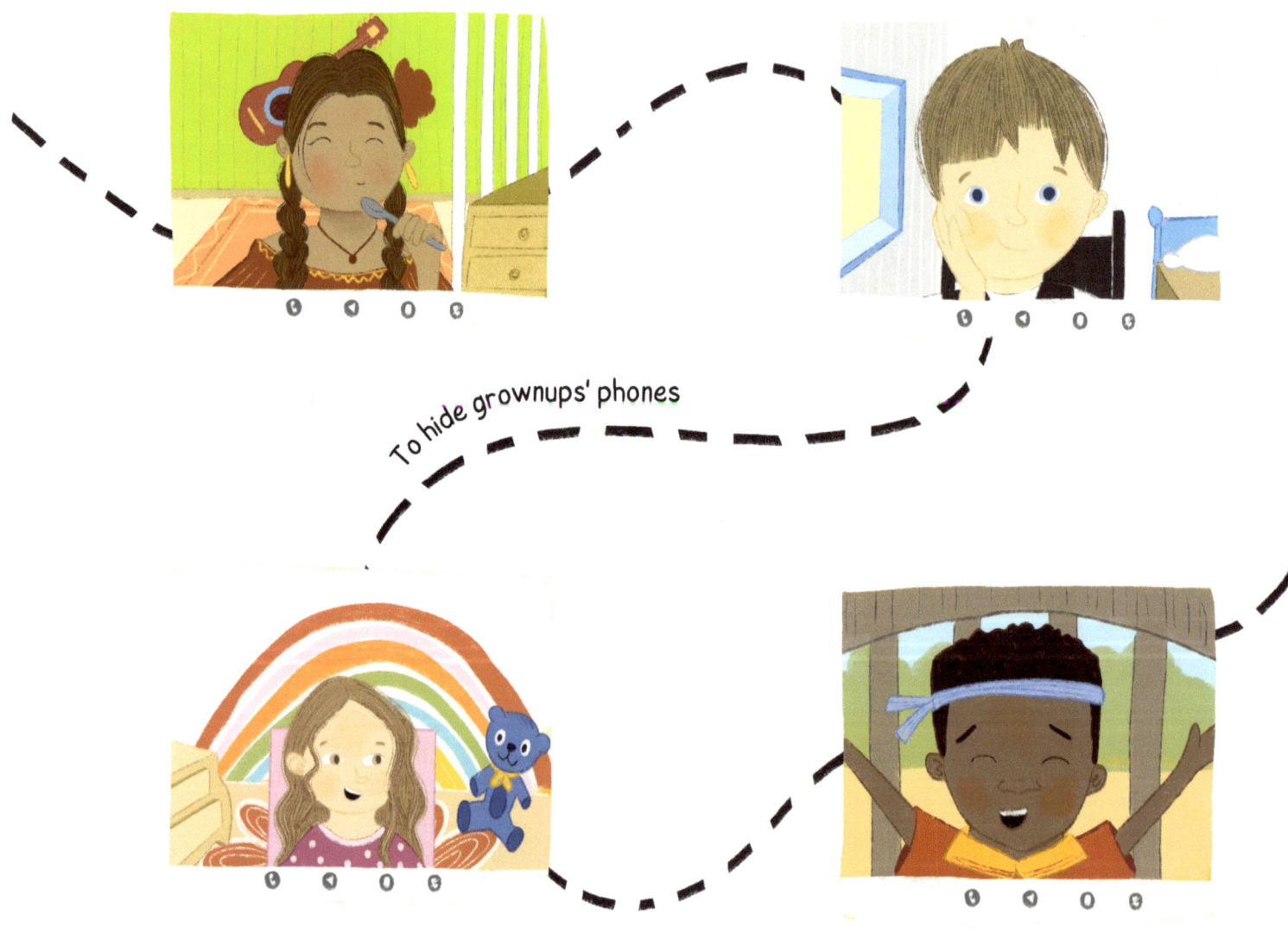

To hide grownups' phones

The world was in mayhem; phones were lost, and phones were found,
But grownups started noticing the beauty all around.

With the children's guidance, they learned about the landmarks' magic,
And how to live in the moment and not be too frantic.

Parents played with their children and explored the Earth,
Nature walks and picnics became of great worth.

Landmarks returned to their original home,
With stories and memories, they had the urge to roam.

Families celebrated their newfound appreciation,

For the world's wonders and magic

without hesitation.

Life went back to normal with a magical twist,
As the landmarks' secrets were no longer missed.

The end!

LET'S LEARN SOME
FACTS

EIFFEL TOWER

The Eiffel Tower in France is a super tall iron giant, as tall as about 81 giraffes standing on top of each other! Every night, it lights up and sparkles like a Christmas tree. It's painted every 7 years to keep it shiny and new. You can even ride an elevator to the top and see all of Paris! Built by a man named Gustave Eiffel, it's been around for over 130 birthdays since it was finished in 1889.

The Eiffel Tower is one of the most popular places in the world, with lots of people visiting every day. And did you know? When it's very windy, the Eiffel Tower can sway a little bit, just like a tall tree!

BIG BEN

Big Ben is a huge clock in London, England—it's one of the most famous clocks in the world! Big Ben is actually the nickname for the bell inside the clock tower, and it weighs as much as 13 small elephants. Every hour, Big Ben chimes and makes a loud "bong" sound that you can hear all over the city.

GOLDEN GATE BRIDGE

The Golden Gate Bridge is a bright red-orange bridge in San Francisco, California, and it's one of the most famous bridges in the world!

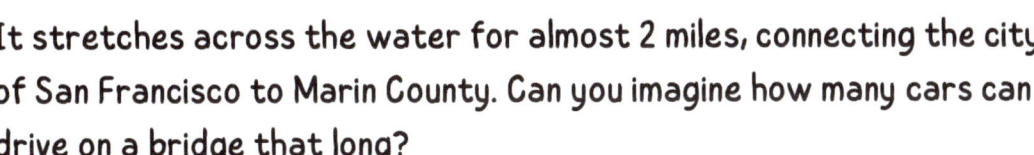

It stretches across the water for almost 2 miles, connecting the city of San Francisco to Marin County. Can you imagine how many cars can drive on a bridge that long?

PARTHENON

The Parthenon is a big, ancient temple in Athens, Greece. It was built a very long time ago, over 2,400 years ago, to honour Athena, the goddess who protected the city.

This amazing temple is made of marble and has tall columns. Even though some parts have broken, it still looks impressive. Inside, there used to be a giant statue of Athena made of gold and ivory!

GREAT WALL OF CHINA

The Great Wall of China is a very, very long wall that winds through mountains and valleys in China. It was built a long time ago to help protect the country from invaders. This amazing structure is so long that if you lined up 500,000 school buses, they would stretch just as far! It's made of stone, bricks, and earth, and it has watchtowers where soldiers used to stand guard.

Did you know that people can walk on the Great Wall and see beautiful views of the mountains and countryside? It's like a giant dragon stretching across the land, watching over China.

THE GREAT SPHINX OF GIZA

The Great Sphinx is a giant statue in Egypt with the body of a lion and the head of a person. It's one of the oldest and most famous statues in the world!

This beautiful statue has a mysterious face that people think might be a pharaoh, which is like an ancient king of Egypt.

Did you know that the Great Sphinx has been standing in the desert for over 4,500 years? It's like a giant guardian, keeping watch over the pyramids and the people of Egypt.

MOUNT EVEREST

Mount Everest is the tallest mountain in the world, and it's located in the Himalayas, between Nepal and China. It's so tall that it reaches up into the clouds!

This amazing mountain is as high as 20 skyscrapers stacked on top of each other. Climbers from all over the world try to reach the top, but it's very hard because it's so high and cold.

NIAGARA FALLS

Niagara Falls is a huge, beautiful waterfall on the border between the United States and Canada. It's made up of three waterfalls that come together to create a lot of rushing water.

This waterfall is so powerful that it can fill up millions of bathtubs every minute! People from all over the world visit Niagara Falls to see the water roar and splash.

LANDMARKS
AROUND THE WORLD

1. El Obelisco-Argentina
2. La Bombonera-Argentina
3. Salvo Palace-Uruguay
4. El Morro de Arica-Chile
5. The Ruins of São Miguel das Missões-Brazil
6. Christ the Redeemer-Brazil
7. The Octavio Frias de Oliveira bridge-Brazil
8. Machu Picchu-Peru
9. The Paseo Los Próceres-Venezuela
10. Cartagena das Índias-Colombia
11. The Monumento a los Héroes de la Restauración-Dominican Republic
12. Chichén Itzá-Mexico
13. Hollywood, Sign-United States
14. Golden Gate Bridge-United States
15. Benny Benson Memorial - Seward, Alaska, United States
16. Mount Ballyhoo - Unalaska, Alaska, United States
17. National Mall-United States
18. Terry Fox Monument-Canada
19. The Mount Rushmore National Memorial-United States.
20. Statue of Liberty-United States
21. Niagara Falls, Ontario, Canada / New York, United States
22. Hallgrimskirkja, Reykjavik-Iceland
23. Hadrian's Wall-England
24. Northeast Greenland National Park-Greenland
25. Brandenburg Gate-Germany
26. Skulptur i Pilane-Sweden
27. Elisabeth Tower (Big Ben)-England
28. Stonehenge-England
29. Angel of the North-England
30. Loch Ness-Scotland
31. Cliffs of Moher-Ireland
32. Louvre Museum, Paris, France
33. Sagrada Familia-Spain
34. The Ben Youssef Madrasa-Morocco
35. Martyrs' Memorial-Algeria
36. Laâyoune - Western Sahara
37. Eiffel Tower Paris-France
38. The Pantheon-Italy
39. Osun Sacred Grove Osogbo-Nigeria
40. Krugersdorp Gauteng Game Reserve-South Africa
41. Independence Square-Mozambique
42. Fahaleovantena Tribes Monument-Madagascar
43. The Askari Monument-Tanzania
44. The Great Sphinx of Giza-Egypt
45. Colosseo (Colosseum)-Italy
46. The Parthenon-Greece
47. The Giza pyramid complex Giza-Egypt
48. Leaning Tower of Pisa-Italy
49. The Bolshoi Theatre-Russia
50. The Motherland Calls-Russia
51. The Kremlin and Red Square-Russia
52. The Taj Mahal-India
53. Kande Vihara Buddha Statue-Sri Lanka
54. The Petronas Towers-Malaysia
55. The Great Wall of China-China
56. The Imperial Palace-Japan
57. The Sydney Opera House-Australia
58. Milford Sound, Fiordland National Park-New Zealand
59. Uluru, Northern Territory-Australia

**Tag Kassi on Social Media.
She would love to hear from you!**

- www.adventuresomewords.com
- drkassi@adventuresomewords.com
- @drkassi
- @authorkassipsifogeorgou

About the Author

Landmarks on the move

Kassi Psifogeorgou is a UK-based children's author and neuroscience-inspired storyteller whose work blends cultural heritage, humour, and behavioural science.

She is the creator of two celebrated series: My Greek Roots, which introduces young readers to Greek culture and traditions with warmth and authenticity, and Grow As You Go, a behavioural-science-based series that helps children navigate emotions and everyday challenges through engaging, research-grounded stories.

Her books have received multiple international awards and achieved bestseller status on Amazon, recognised for their originality, emotional intelligence, and inclusive approach. Through her writing, Kassi champions diversity and cultural representation, offering young readers stories that honour identity, belonging, and cross-cultural understanding.

Her work has been showcased at the Greek Embassy in London, and her titles have been approved by the Ministry of Education, Sport and Youth of Cyprus for inclusion in student libraries.

Follow Laura on Social Media.
       She would love to hear from you!

◉ @lauramocelinart

ⓕ @laauramocelin

✉ contato@lauramocelin.com

About the Illustrator

I'm Laura Mocelin, illustrator and architect living in the north of Rio Grande do Sul, Brasil. I was born in 1996 in Santa Catarina and since then I introduced art in my life in many different ways.

My graduation in architecture and urbanism helped a lot to develop myself as an artist, especially regarding to space, time and dimensions. I always liked to draw on paper, with paint and brushes. But digital art won my heart due to the immense amount of possibilities it gives artists, besides allowing for a more in depth study of light, color and stroke. Today I illustrate mainly children's books, which take me back to my childhood and make me see life in a different way.

MEET THE SKY SIBLINGS

"Rain, Cloud, and Wind aren't ordinary children; they're the Knights of the Changing Skies. When they argue, snow falls, storms rage, and autumn winds roar. But when they laugh and get along, spring blossoms and summer shines brighter than ever."

A story about **growth mindset**

Mr Pizza is a plain slice—just cheese and crust. Nothing fancy at all. At first, Mr Pizza feels a bit lost in a world of flashy toppings.

But when others invite him to play, something surprising happens—olives become buttons, mushrooms form a bow tie, and spinach turns into a moustache. Bit by bit, Mr Pizza discovers he truly belongs.

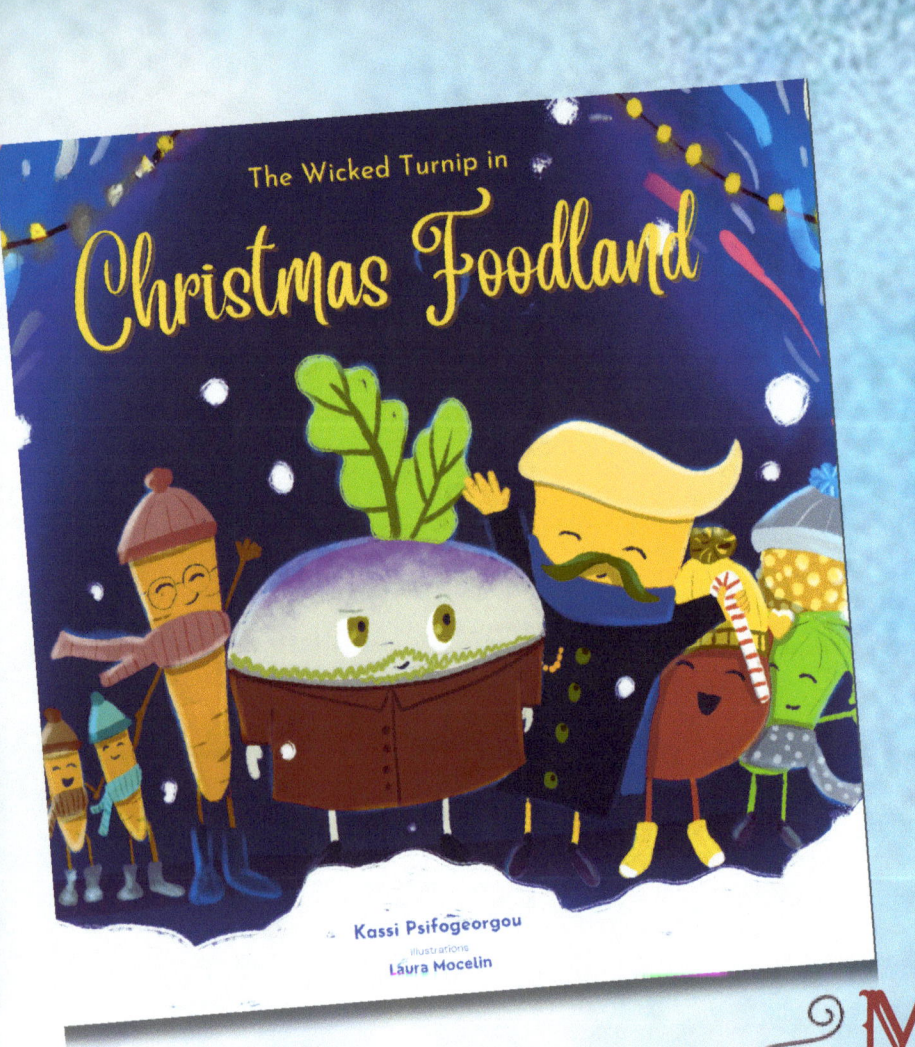

FOLLOW THE MISCHIEF IN FOODLAND

CAN ONE GRUMPY VEG HELP CHRISTMAS AFTER ALL?

You Might Also Like

On Amazon

Our Very Greek Easter: A very Orthodox Easter
STORY MONSTERS APPROVED

*** Tom's family is flying to Greece for Easter to visit Yiayia, Papou and the rest of their extended family. He's so excited to get acquainted with all the Greek traditions of the Holy Week. So, he writes a letter to his best friend describing what he and his brothers did every day, starting from Lazarus Saturday to Easter Sunday.***

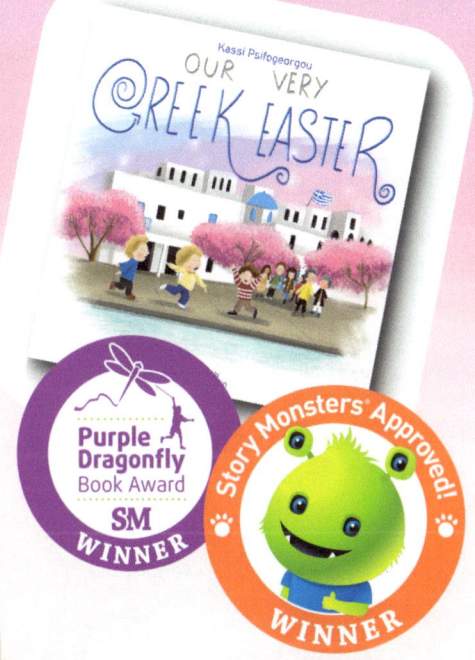

Travel to Greece through this gorgeously illustrated book and learn about the Holy Week in Greek Culture from a Christian perspective. Read about the wonderful traditions that still carry on and the delicious Greek meals planned for the special days!

This book is a keepsake gift that children can enjoy all over the world, focused on the Greek Orthodox Easter.

Our Very Greek Summer: And a very Greek Baptism

Alina and her mom have been invited to a baptism in Greece over the summer by their close friends, the Papadopoulos family.

Get ready for an enchanting journey through this stunningly illustrated story, and read about world-famous Greek hospitality! Learn about a traditional Greek baptism, from the godparents' important role to the celebratory feast and dancing called "gledi".

This book is a keepsake gift that children can enjoy all over the world, focused on the Greek 'philoxenia' and the Greek Orthodox Baptism.

On Amazon

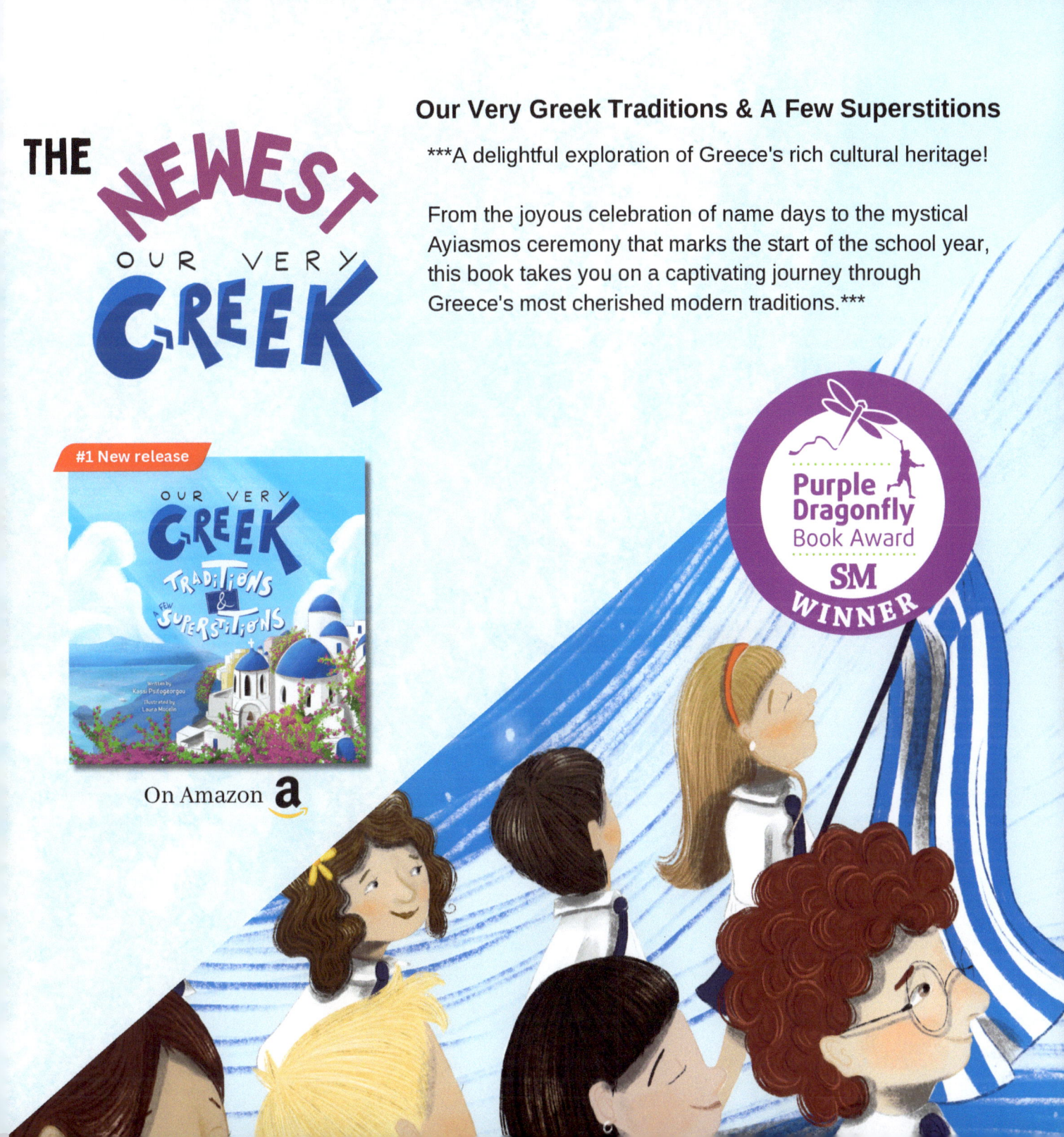